Grandad

a

Seawee entre

CW01604165

Illustrated by Val Biro

Ginn

W.G. BRINY'S
World Famous
SEAWEED
GARDEN
CENTRE
371 Varieties.
Inspection invited.
BRING YOUR OWN
Diving Equipment

"I don't really like porridge," he told Grandad Briny, "but Mum says it's good for me."

"Tell her to cook it in cabbage water with a dollop of mustard – improves the flavour no end," Grandad said. "Now, I'm going out in the submarine. Want to come?"

"Yes, please, Grandad!" He raced upstairs.

"Grandad says I can go out in the submarine with him – can I, Mum?"

"I suppose so," Mum sighed. "Don't get wet."

Billy snatched up his wet suit and flippers and rushed downstairs again.

"Hurry up, the sea horses will be wanting their feed," Grandad said, grabbing a packet of seakale from the kitchen cupboard.

"I think the octopuses are up to something," Grandad said, as they went down the stone steps to the cave. "They're always hanging round the Seaweed Garden Centre, talking to the sea horses when they're working."

"What do they want?" Billy asked.

"I don't know, but I don't trust them. They're mad about my Exotic Black seaweed – it's their favourite supper dish. I give them some in exchange for sea anemones, you know."

They climbed aboard the submarine and Grandad gave Billy a wodge of giddy gum to chew.

"Right," said Grandad. "Wet suit ON! Flippers ON! Giddy gum CHEW!"

"Han I shtere?" Billy asked, chewing hard.

"Yesh. Ninehy nine noreasht," Grandad mumbled.

Billy steered the submarine 99 degrees north-east, to the floor of the cave. It stopped by the starfish rocks and the crab pool.

"Re'y?" Grandad asked, giving a last chew on his gum. *"Blow!"*

The giddy gum was a special invention of Grandad's. It was always full of air so that they could breathe under water. They blew until the giddy bubbles were big enough to go over their heads, then they climbed out of the submarine. To his surprise, Billy saw that there were no starfish on the rocks, and the anemones were all closed up.

"H'm," Grandad said in a wavery, underwater sort of voice, "where have those dratted starfish got to?"

Billy scrambled over the rocks. The starfish were huddled together in a deep, dark pool.

"I think they're frightened of something," Billy said. "They're all shivery."

"Odd," Grandad said, "there are no crabs in the crab pool either. CRABS! Where are you?"

The sand at the bottom of the crab pool began to move as the crabs popped up from under it.

"What in the world are you hiding for?" Grandad said crossly. "It's time you were helping the sea horses get ready for work."

But the crabs just scuttled around and waved their feelers about. They seemed to be pointing towards the stables that Grandad had made at the side of the cave for the sea horses.

Quickly, Billy and Grandad Briny went to the stables. They were empty. All the sea horses had disappeared!

CHAPTER 2: "Our sea horses are missing!"

"Perhaps they've gone to the Seaweed Garden Centre," Billy said.

"We'd better go and look," said Grandad.

Grandad Briny's Seaweed Garden Centre was world famous. (There was a notice board in front of Billy's house which said so!) He grew 371 different sorts of seaweed, which he prepared for the market himself. Most of it was sold by mail order, and the chefs of all the best restaurants bought his Special Purple seaweed for making soup.

Chemists bought his Green Spotted
seaweed to make into medicines.

The sea horses worked in the Garden Centre, helping Grandad with the ploughing and harvesting. This morning though, they were not there.

"Oh, Grandad!" Billy exclaimed. "You said about the octopuses – do you think they could have taken the sea horses?"

"I don't know," Grandad said grimly, "but we're going to find them. Back to the submarine, Billy!"

When they reached the open sea, Grandad asked some passing winkles if they'd seen the sea horses. But the winkles just winked at them and

didn't say a word. A gang of cheeky shrimps swam round the submarine, pulling faces at them through the glass sides. Billy screwed up his nose and pressed it against the glass. The shrimps swam away, grinning.

Suddenly, the submarine began to rock up and down. Then it rocked from side to side.

"Is it an earthquake?" Billy asked, hoping he didn't sound too scared.

"What?" Grandad was busy trying to steer. "No, just a sea serpent."

And there he was, an enormous sea serpent, swimming lazily through the water, his great shining blue-green body making swirly patterns as sand, small fish and shells were scattered by the churning sea.

"Hi! You there – sea serpent!" Grandad Briny shouted. "Have you seen our sea horses anywhere – or some octopuses?"

The sea serpent looked thoughtful. "Octopuses," he said slowly, as though trying to remember what an octopus was, "and – what was the other thing?"

"Sea horses."

"Ah, yes, sea horses. You mean the ones the octopuses took to their grotto last night? Between you and me, I don't think the sea horses really wanted to go."

"But – what did they take them for?"

"Oh, to harvest their seaweed. Personally, I don't think it's quite ripe yet, but you know how impatient octopuses are."

"Just a minute," Grandad said slowly, "what seaweed are we talking about?"

"Exotic Black, I think they called it. They said you were too stingy to let them have enough of yours, so they decided to grow their own."

"So that's what they were up to in the Garden Centre!" Grandad exploded. "They were trying to find out how to grow it." He suddenly

looked serious. "I don't like the sound of this. If it's harvested before it's ripe it could make them ill."

"They seemed to be all right this morning," the sea serpent remarked. "I think they were having a fancy dress party. Some of the octopuses were wearing pink and yellow outfits – quite pretty I thought."

"Pink and yellow octopuses!" Grandad exclaimed. "I think we'd better see what's going on."

"I'll take you," said the sea serpent.

The submarine gave a shudder as Grandad held grimly on to the steering wheel and followed him.

Chapter 3: Pink and yellow octopuses?

The sea serpent led them to a grotto beneath a rock far out to sea.

As they left the submarine they saw the sea horses at once. They were swimming around at the back of the grotto, surrounded by a ring of – pink and yellow octopuses!

Billy and Grandad yelled with laughter. There was no danger of being overheard, because the rest of the grotto was filled with black octopuses, all laughing and jeering and pointing at their unfortunate companions.

"Whatever are they dressed up like that for?" Billy chuckled.

"They aren't dressed up, Billy." Grandad stopped laughing rather suddenly. "They've come out in pink and yellow spots!"

Billy looked more closely. Grandad was right. Some of the octopuses had trails of small spots all over them, others had some small spots and some big ones, and some were covered in big pink and yellow blotches!

There was still a small patch of Exotic Black seaweed growing at one side of the grotto. Grandad went to look at it.

"No wonder they've come out in spots, greedy things," he growled. "It isn't ripe. And they don't know how to prepare it. If you put in too much cochinocredyne – or not enough salts of urticarium – you don't get a first class seaweed supper. It's a good job they didn't all eat it."

"They must think it's the sea horses' fault they've come out in spots," Billy said anxiously. "I hope they don't hurt them."

The pink and yellow octopuses were angry and itchy. They kept lashing out at the sea horses with their tentacles. But the sea horses seemed to think it was a game; they just grinned and avoided the tentacles quite easily.

"Time to take them home, I think," Grandad said. "Round them up, Billy."

"Can we have our sea horses back please?" Billy asked, shouting to make himself heard.

There was a sudden silence as all the black octopuses stopped laughing. Then they glared angrily at Billy and Grandad and began to swim towards them.

"I – er – think we're going to need some help," Grandad said. They raced out of the grotto and hid behind the sea serpent, who was dozing beside the submarine.

"Perhaps the sea serpent would help us?" Billy whispered.

"Excellent suggestion, boy," said Grandad. "We'll wake him up and ask."

Chapter 4:
Sea serpent to the rescue

It took the sea serpent a little while to remember where he was.

"Ah, yes, sea horses," he said, with a yawn that rocked the submarine like a tidal wave. "You'd like them back?"

"Yes, please," Billy said. "The octopuses looked so cross."

"Well, I could tell them a story," the sea serpent said. "My stories often send people to sleep. Then you could creep in and rescue them."

"It's worth a try," Grandad said.

They hid among the rocks while the sea serpent went into the grotto, and presently they heard his drowsy voice telling a story about a river winding in and out among the meadows and woods, making waterfalls over rocks, dancing and bubbling down to the sea …

Billy and Grandad yawned.

The sea serpent's voice stopped at last, and they crept into the grotto. The sea serpent was curled up in a ball, with the octopuses coiled around him, snoring gently.

Billy bravely crept past the sleeping octopuses and shook the nearest sea horse. "We've come to rescue you," he whispered.

Silently, all the sea horses followed Billy out of the grotto.

"Now, swim for your lives!" Grandad Briny ordered.

By the time Grandad and Billy got back to the cave the sea horses had returned to their stables and were being fussed over by the crabs and groomed by the starfish. Billy filled their nosebags with the seakale they should have had for breakfast.

"Time for lunch, I think," Grandad announced, when they got back to his basement.

Billy shouted up the stairs. "Mum! Can I stay here for lunch? Grandad said I could."

"Oh, very well," Mum sighed. "Don't eat too much, now."

They had fried gulls eggs with gravy and marshmallows, and whelks in chocolate sauce for afters.

"Well," said Grandad Briny, wiping his chin. "I suppose we'd better go and sort out those silly octopuses now."

"And thank the sea serpent for his help," Billy reminded him.

When they got back to the grotto, they found the sea serpent still entangled with the octopuses.

"There's a small problem," the sea serpent said. "I told them my 'winding and gliding' river story, and unfortunately there isn't really enough room in the grotto for them to join in the actions, so we've got ourselves a bit tied up. We can't untangle ourselves."

Grandad and Billy went to look. Sure enough, the octopuses were very firmly stuck!

Chapter 5: Black treacle oil

"When the chain on my bike got stuck Dad put some oil on it," Billy said helpfully. "Perhaps if we oil the octos we can get them unstuck."

"Good idea, Billy," Grandad said. "We'll go home and get some!"

"Mum's just bought a horrible great bottle of cod liver oil – to see me through the winter, she says. We might use that, I don't mind," Billy said hopefully.

"Just the thing," said Grandad. "Nip up and get it."

"Cod liver oil for sea serpents?" Mum sighed. "Whatever next?"

"I'm not sure that will be enough," Grandad said. "I've got a big jar of black treacle. If we mix them together, that should do."

It made a thick, smelly mixture, and it was hard work rubbing it into the tight knot of octopuses and sea serpent. But after a while the sea serpent gave a mighty heave, and shook himself free of the octopuses.

"Grandad –" Billy whispered.

"Just a minute, lad," Grandad said. "Now listen, you octopuses! Before we unscramble you – I want your word that you won't interfere with my sea horses again. Or try to grow Exotic Black seaweed!"

The octopuses nodded their heads.

"Grandad –" Billy whispered again.

"Work first, chat afterwards," Grandad said. He rubbed the black treacle mixture vigorously into the octopuses. Before long they were all untangled, and waving their tentacles about to get the feeling back into them. The pink and yellow spots were beginning to fade as well.

"Now, what was it you wanted to say?" Grandad asked Billy.

"Look at the sea serpent," Billy whispered. "I don't think he's noticed yet, but he's got black patches all over him."

"Oh-oh," Grandad muttered, "I think it's time we went home."

The next day, no one seemed very keen to go out of the cave. The crabs scuttled about cleaning the cave floor, the starfish swept out the stables and Billy and Grandad were working in the Garden Centre when the sea serpent swam into the cave.

"If you've come about the black patches, I can explain –" Grandad began.

"Elegant, aren't they?" the sea serpent interrupted. "They set off my blue and green scales charmingly, don't you think? Actually, I've come to ask a favour. My sister's quite jealous – I shan't have a minute's peace until I get some of your wonderful black treacle oil for her too. Oh yes, and the octopuses say they've gone off seaweed, but they'd like some of that oil – it makes their skins all soft and shiny! So we wondered if you could supply us on a regular basis?"

"I think that could be arranged," Grandad said. "Now, let me see – three litres of cod liver oil to 800 grams of black treacle. Mix well and multiply by …" He took his calculator out of his pocket.

"Do you think you can trust the octopuses now, Grandad?" Billy asked.

"Oh, I think so," said Grandad Briny with a grin. "If they don't behave, I can always put some pink and yellow colouring in the treacle oil and bring them out in stripes, can't I?"